Handmade
HOLIDAY CRAFTS

Handmade EASTER Crafts

By Ruth Owen

Gareth Stevens
PUBLISHING

Please visit our website, www.garethstevens.com. For a free color catalog of all
our high-quality books, call toll free 1-800-542-2595 or fax 1-877-542-2596.

Cataloging-in-Publication Data
Names: Owen, Ruth.
Title: Handmade Easter crafts / Ruth Owen.
Description: New York : Gareth Stevens Publishing, 2017. | Series: Handmade holiday crafts |
  Includes index.
Identifiers: ISBN 9781482460834 (pbk.) | ISBN 9781482461565 (library bound) |
  ISBN 9781482460841 (6 pack)
Subjects: LCSH: Easter decorations--Juvenile literature. | Handicraft--Juvenile literature.
Classification: LCC TT900.E2 O84 2017 | DDC 745.594'1--dc23

Published in 2017 by
Gareth Stevens Publishing
111 East 14th Street, Suite 349
New York, NY 10003

First Edition

Produced for Gareth Stevens Publishing by Ruby Tuesday Books Ltd
Designer: Emma Randall

Photo Credits: Courtesy of Ruby Tuesday Books and Shutterstock.

Printed in the United States of America
CPSIA compliance information: Batch CW17GS:
For further information contact Gareth Stevens, New York, New York at 1-800-542-2595.

CONTENTS

A HAPPY HANDMADE EASTER

When Easter comes around, the stores are filled with tempting treats and lovely holiday decorations and gifts. Sometimes, however, it can be expensive to buy these items.

This year, try the projects in this book and you'll soon be making your own gifts and **traditional** Easter egg decorations. All you need are inexpensive crafting supplies and scraps of **recycled** materials from around your home.

Follow the instructions, throw in a little of your own **creativity**, and you'll soon be having a very happy handmade Easter!

STAY SAFE

It's very important to have an adult around whenever you do any of the following tasks:

- Use scissors
- Use a glue gun
- Use a stove
- Use a knife

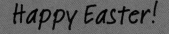
Happy Easter!

YOU WILL NEED:

To make the projects in this book, you don't need any special equipment—just some basic crafting tools and supplies.

- Scissors
- Glue gun
- White glue
- Paints and paintbrushes
- Stapler
- A black marker
- Glue stick
- A ruler
- A hole punch
- A kabob skewer

POPSICLE STICK CHICK EASTER CARDS

Say "Happy Easter!" to your family and friends with these adorable Easter chick handmade greeting cards made from popsicle sticks.

YOU WILL NEED:

To make one greeting card
- 5 popsicle sticks
- Yellow paint + paintbrush
- A piece of colorful card stock
- White glue
- Yellow + orange card stock
- Peel-and-stick googly eyes

Paint five popsicle sticks with yellow paint and allow to dry thoroughly.

1

2 Fold the piece of colored card stock in half to make a greeting card. Glue the five yellow sticks to the front of the card.

3 Cut two wing shapes from the yellow card stock.

4 Cut two feet and a triangular beak from the orange card stock.

Happy Easter!

5 Glue the wings and feet to the card. Tuck them slightly under the popsicle sticks.

6 Glue the beak to the popsicle sticks and add the googly eyes.

7 Use a marker to add a greeting to your Easter card.

CONFETTI EGGS

Do you enjoy painting eggs at Easter? This year fill some eggs with handmade, recycled confetti and have fun cracking them over your friends' heads!

YOU WILL NEED:

- Eggs
- Kabob skewer
- Dishwashing detergent and warm water
- Paper towels
- Paper scraps
- A hole punch
- Paint and paintbrushes
- A teaspoon
- Colored tissue paper
- Scissors
- White glue

1 Carefully use the kabob skewer to poke a small hole in the end of an egg. Then, using your fingers, gently break a small hole in the shell about the size of a dime.

Hole the size of a dime.

2 Use the skewer to very gently stir up the egg, to break up the yolk. Drain the egg and rinse out the eggshell with dishwashing detergent and warm water.

Gently dab the eggshell dry with a paper towel and leave somewhere warm to dry thoroughly.

 Make your recycled confetti using a hole punch. You can use scraps of colored paper, old wrapping paper, and even magazines.

When your eggshells are dry, have fun painting and decorating them. Allow them to dry thoroughly.

 Use the teaspoon to carefully spoon confetti into the eggs.

Finally glue a small square of colored tissue paper over the hole in the egg to seal in the confetti.

Have fun cracking your eggs and sprinkling confetti over your friends!

POM-POM BUNNIES GARLAND

This Easter, decorate your home with a cute **garland** of Easter bunnies with handmade yarn pom-pom tails.

YOU WILL NEED:

- Tracing paper
- A pencil
- Scissors
- Colored or patterned thin cardboard
- String for hanging
- A glue gun
- Yarn in your choice of colors
- A fork

1 Begin by tracing the bunny shape on this page. Cut out the shape and use it as a template.

2 To make your card bunnies, lay the tracing paper template on the reverse side of the colored cardboard and draw around it. Cut out the bunnies.

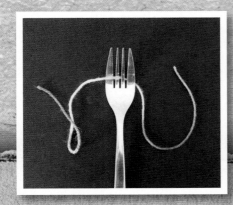

3 To make a yarn pom-pom tail for a bunny, you will need a fork.

4 Take a piece of yarn that's about 6 inches (15 cm) long, and thread it through the center of the fork.

5 Now begin winding yarn around the tines of the fork.

Tines

Wind the yarn around the fork about 40 to 50 times.

6 Take hold of the strand of yarn that you placed between the center tines of the fork and tie it tightly in a double knot around the rest of the yarn.

Loops of yarn

Loops of yarn

Center strand of yarn tied in a double knot.

7 Slide the yarn off the fork. You will now have a small bunch of yarn with loops on either side of the tightly knotted center strand of yarn

8 Carefully snip through the loops on one side of the bunch of yarn.

Then cut through the loops on the other side.

9 Trim off any remaining long pieces of yarn and fluff out your pom-pom. You can make pom-pom tails in white or your choice of color.

10 Use the glue gun to stick the pom-pom tails to the cardboard bunnies.

Finally, glue the bunnies to a string for hanging.

YARN EGGS

All you need to make these decorative eggs is some balloons, yarn, and white glue. You will get a little messy, but it's worth it!

YOU WILL NEED:

- Newspaper
- Balloons
- Shallow dish
- A 50/50 mixture of white glue and water
- Scissors
- Yarn or embroidery thread in your choice of colors
- A dressmaking pin

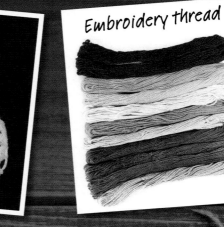

Embroidery thread

Yarn

1. To make this project, use a wipe-clean surface or cover your work surface with sheets of newspaper.

2. Blow up a balloon, so it is around 3 to 4 inches (8–10 cm) long and tie it off.

Gently pull and manipulate the balloon to make it egg-shaped.

3. Cut around 6 to 8 strands of yarn that are about 36 inches (91 cm) long.

4. Mix white glue and water in equal parts in a shallow dish.

5 Soak the strands of yarn in the glue mixture.

6 Pull a strand of yarn from the dish and drape and wind it around the balloon. The yarn will cling or stick to the balloon. Gently press on the ends of the yarn to get them to stick to the balloon's surface.

7 Continue winding and draping strands of yarn around the balloon until you've created a pattern and effect that you like.

8 Leave the eggs to dry on a sheet of newspaper in a warm place. As the yarn dries, it will become stiff. On a warm, dry day, you can also hang your eggs outdoors to dry.

If you leave some gaps between the yarn strands, you can pop mini chocolate eggs into your yarn egg once it's dried, and give the egg as a gift.

 9 When a yarn egg is dry and hard, pop the balloon with a pin. Carefully pull the pieces of burst balloon from the egg.

 **10** Your yarn balloons can be displayed in bowls, hung up, or given as Easter gifts.

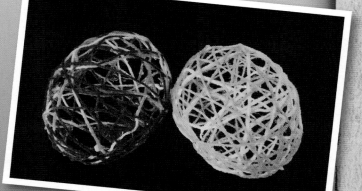

WOVEN EASTER BASKETS

It wouldn't be Easter without Easter baskets and egg hunts. So have fun making these woven baskets that can be made from colorful construction paper or thin cardboard.

YOU WILL NEED:

- Construction paper or thin cardboard; we used sheets of paper that were 8 inches by 12 inches (20 x 30.5 cm)
- A ruler
- Scissors
- A stapler

1 Begin by choosing two sheets of paper or cardboard in contrasting colors.

Don't worry if every strip isn't perfectly straight. It won't show when the basket is complete!

2 Cut the paper into strips that are 1 inch (2.5 cm) wide.

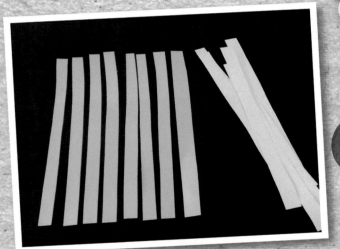

3 Lay out eight strips in one color (green) on a flat surface. Leave a little space between each strip.

4 Now weave a strip of paper in a contrasting color (yellow) through the eight strips, weaving under, over, under, over, etc.

5 Now weave a second yellow strip through the green strips.

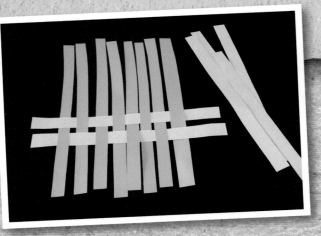

The first two strips (yellow) can be a little tricky as the flat strips (green) will move around. Once you have two cross strips in place, however, the woven paper will become more rigid and manageable.

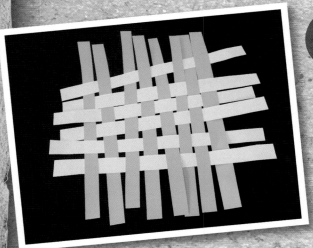

6 Continue weaving yellow strips through the green strips until you've created a square of woven strips to be the base of the basket.

Gently nudge and slide the strips together to tighten up the weave.

7 Now make sure the unwoven strips on all four sides of the square are equal length. Carefully pull on them if you need to adjust the lengths.

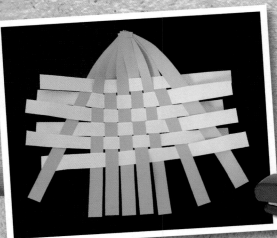

8 To create the shape of the basket, gather together the green strips on one side of the square and staple them.

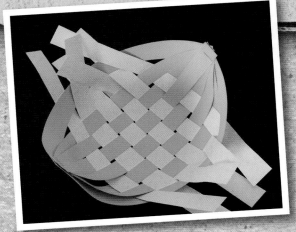

9 Repeat with the green strips on the other side of the square.

You will notice that this causes the woven section to curl up and create a basket shape.

10 Now gather together the yellow strips in the same way and staple them. The base of the basket is complete.

11 Take a strip in each color and staple them across the basket to form a handle.

12 To make a bow for the handle, make a loop from a paper strip and then staple the loop through its center.

Repeat with a second strip.

13 Staple the loops to the center of the basket's handle.

Happy Egg Hunting!

EASTER WREATH

This lovely paper **wreath** looks complicated, but it's actually very easy to make. Hang it inside your home, or if the weather is dry, hang it on your front door to welcome Easter visitors.

YOU WILL NEED:

- A piece of thick cardboard
- A dinner plate and a small bowl
- A marker
- Scissors
- Construction paper
- A stapler
- A glue stick
- A small piece of ribbon

1 To make a frame for the wreath, place a dinner plate on the cardboard. Draw around it with a marker.

Then place a small bowl in the center of the circle you've just drawn. You will now have a doughnut shape. Cut out the shape.

2 Cut the colored paper into strips that are 8 inches (20 cm) long and 1 inch (2.5 cm) wide.

To cover the wreath frame you will need 36 strips of paper.

3 Make the paper strips into loops and staple them.

Make the wreath in springlike colors such as pink, green, blue, and yellow.

4 Now begin gluing the paper loops to the frame in the pattern as shown.

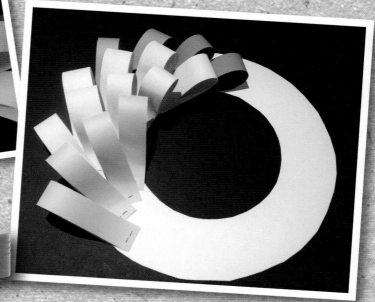

5 Keep adding loops until the cardboard frame is covered.

Slide the last four loops under the first four to complete the pattern.

First four loops

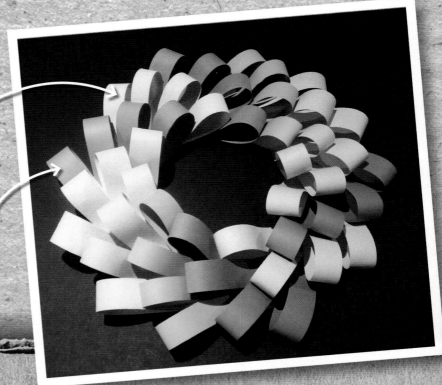

6 To complete the wreath, glue or staple a small loop of ribbon to the back of the wreath frame for hanging.

HATCHING CHICKS

YOU WILL NEED:

- Eggs (one or two per person)
- A pan
- Water
- A large carrot (this will make up to 6 hatching chicks)
- A knife and cutting board
- A kabob skewer
- Shredded wheat

This final project doesn't just look good, it's also good to eat! You will need to allow 24 hours to make your hatching chicks.

Make sure you follow good **hygiene** practices by washing your hands before working on this project.

1 Cook your hard-boiled eggs on the day before you want to use them.

2 Put the eggs into a pan of cold water and bring it to a boil. Allow the water to boil for about 10 minutes, then turn off the heat. Leave the pan to cool for at least an hour, or until the water is cool.

3 Drain the water and put the eggs into the refrigerator overnight. Chilling the eggs will make them easier to peel.

Make sure an adult is nearby or helps you when you're boiling the eggs and chopping the carrot.

4 Carefully peel the shells from the eggs, and place to one side.

5 Wash and peel the carrot.

6 Cut thin circles of carrot. Then cut the circles into quarters to make the chicks' feet.

7 Cut two thin lengths of carrot to make the legs for each chick.

Pair of feet

Pair of legs

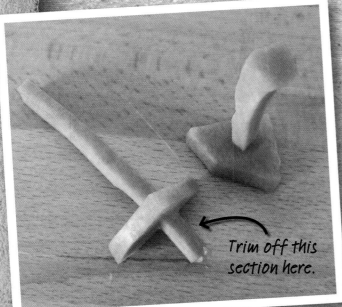

Trim off this section here.

8 Take two quarters of carrot and carefully pierce a hole in each one using a kabob skewer. The hole needs to be big enough for a carrot leg to fit into.

9 Push a leg through the hole. Trim off the excess.

Now make two leg holes in each egg using the skewer. The holes should be slightly smaller than the thickness of the carrot legs, so that when you push the legs into the egg it will be a good, tight fit.

Make leg holes here

To serve your eggs, crumble up shredded wheat or another cereal to make a nest. Place your chicks into their nest and serve!

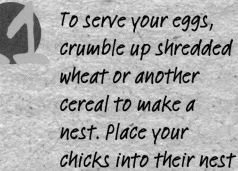

GLOSSARY

creativity
The use of imagination or original ideas to create something new and unusual.

garland
A length of flowers, leaves, bows, or other items that are strung together and hung up as a decoration.

hygiene
Things that you do to keep yourself or your surroundings clean and free of germs in order to have good health.

recycled
Objects or materials that have been turned into something new instead of being thrown away.

traditional
A way of thinking, behaving, or doing something that a group of people have followed for a long time. For example, going on an egg hunt is traditional at Easter.

wreath
A doughnut-shaped decoration made of flowers, leaves, or other items that is hung on a door.

INDEX

FURTHER INFORMATION

BOOKS:

Brooke, Jasmine. *Origami for Easter*. New York, NY: PowerKids Press, 2017.

Lim, Annalees. *Easter Crafts*. New York, NY: Windmill Books, 2016.

WEBSITES:

Easter Crafts
https://family.disney.com/easter-crafts/
Visit this site to find more fun and festive crafts to make for Easter!